P9-CFU-330

FROM
D.O.C.
TO
C.E.O.

JEMELL "CASPER" HILL

TeamSuccess Publications, L.L.C.

Copyright © 2015 Jemell "Casper" Hill

All rights reserved, including the right to reproduce this book or portions hereof in any form whatsoever without written permission.

Note: Sale of this book without a front cover may be unauthorized. If this book was purchased without a cover, it may have been reported to the publisher as "unsold" or "destroyed," neither the author nor the publisher may have received payment for the sale of this book.

TEAM SUCCESS PUBLICATIONS, LLC
PO Box 2553
York, PA 17405

jjhillionaire@gmail.com
www.facebook.com/casper.hill.12
www.instagram.com/author_casperhill

ISBN-13:   978-0-692-54516-4

Credits:
Written by: Jemell "Casper" Hill
Cover Photographer: © Linda Day
Cover Concept: www.HotBookCovers.com

This book is dedicated to the fallen street generals that I was blessed to have shared time and space with before their unfortunate passing: Mark "SKI" Smith, Bobby "BJ" Greer, Ribat Austin, Dollar Bill, Kevin "Kev-Boogie" Blackwood, Raymond "RAY-Z" Simmons, and more.

Y'all will never be forgotten.

R.I.P. 4 EVER

ACKNOWLEDGEMENTS

First and foremost, to God be the Glory. Father God I am absolutely certain that I am only here today because you had your hand on my life. Without your omnipotent hand on my life, this journey of mine would have concluded a long time ago. I know that I have been divinely favored and for that reason, I am eternally grateful.

To my Beautiful Mother, Gail Hill. You are nothing less than a Phenomenal Mother and Woman. You gave me your unwavering love and support on all five of my jail bids. I Love You beyond comprehension.

To my Father, Jesse "Sugar Pop" Green and my Stepfather Kitt "Big AB" Hamilton, I sincerely thank the both of you. The two of you helped shape me into the man of morals that I am today and the both of you always held me down. I Love Y'all.

To my siblings: Kareem "Stinky" Hill, I Love You Kicko. When you come home, we are taking it even further in Corporate America. To my Sissy Shanita Hill, I Love You beyond words. My Brother Shannon, I Love You. My Brother Devon, I Love You even though you're the one sibling that drives me crazy. Tiante, I Love You Sis. Greg keep holding it down Bro.

To My Beautiful Lady Edquina, Loving You truly is food for my soul. I thank God for you my Queen. TeamSuccess.

To my Amazing Children: Jemell "Young J. Hillionaire" I Love You. Armani Hill my youngest boy, I Love You. Jemela Hill, my princess, I Love You. Jemell Cruz and Kevontre Hill, I know that as a result of me being in and out of jail our relationship isn't the best, but I still have a place in my heart for the both of you.
To my family: Green's, Bethea's, Hill's, Watkin's, Harris', Mitchell's, and Wright's, I Love Y'all. It's way too many of my family members to name everyone individually (Please Understand).

To My Business Comrades: Antoine "Inch" Thomas and my 848 Web Series Family, Jeral "Jamie-O" Jones and Wealth Nation, Wynn Kearse and Wynn Enterprises, Walter "Red" Randall and the Split Your Wig Brand, Raymond "Fresh" Wilson, Lionel "QuietStorm" Weathers, Jamiel Alexander, and Shawn "Bear" Heuston. Anyone that I forgot to mention, please blame my mind and not my heart.

To all my family and friend from Edenwald Projects: This was extremely hard for me because I want to thank all of my peoples in every single building in Edenwald individually, but it's way too many of y'all to name for this little book. Please know that I am grateful and thankful for so many of y'all. Edenwald has loved me, encouraged me, educated me, toughened me up, and supported me and has done so much for me. I love my hood and will never forget my hood, the infamous Edenwald Projects.

To My New York Family and Friends: I love y'all and I miss y'all. I'm honored to be from the most resourceful and most beautiful city in the world. We are so fly.

To My York, PA Family, Friends, and Business Owners: It may be a small city, but it's filled with big-hearted go getters. I'm thankful to have met so many wonderful people. I got a lot of love for y'all. To all my brothers and participants of the "My Brother's Keeper" Program, let's do this. #ILoveYorkCity.

To My Peoples around The World: I was blessed to have met so many wonderful and real people in numerous states. I can't name y'all all in this little book, but please know that I thank God for y'all and got love for y'all. It's TeamSuccess forever.

TABLE OF CONTENTS

AUTHOR BACKGROUND

Born: November 5, 1973, Harlem Hospital

Parents: Jesse "Sugar Pop" Green and Gail Hill

Siblings: Kareem "Stinky" Hill, Shanita Hill, Devon Leath,

                Shannon Leath, Latoya Leath

Raised: Bronx, NY (Edenwald Projects)

First Arrest: November 1992 – Possession of a Controlled

                Substance (My first trip to Rikers Island. Posted

                bail one hour later and was eventually sentenced to

                the ACD Program)

First Bid: Possession of a Firearm. Sentenced to serve 1 year

                on Rikers Island. Served 8 months and was released

                on February 25, 1996

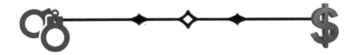

KEYS TO SUCCESS

There are four rungs on the ladder to success:

- **Plan Purposefully**
- **Prepare Prayerfully**
- **Proceed Positively**
- **Pursue Persistently**

Plan Purposefully: I simply can't stress to you enough how important it is for you to understand your specific purpose in life. You can't hit a target that you can't identify. Once you realize what your purpose is, then you formulate a detailed plan to manifest that purpose. There's an old saying "The only thing worse than a man dying like a coward, is a man living without a purpose." Discover your purpose and go for yours.

Prepare Prayerfully: I'm truly a firm believer of the old saying "Never underestimate the power of a plan and a prayer." Regardless of what your religious beliefs are, you have to be spiritually connected and in tune with your higher power. That way as you pray for strength and guidance and live righteously, your journey to success will be blessed.

Proceed Positively: According to the universal "Law of Attraction," it states that like attracts like. You invariably attract into your life people and situations in harmony with your dominant thoughts. Trust and believe, that as long as your product is legal and you conduct yourself in a positive manner, people will gravitate in your direction, eager to help. Closed doors will now suddenly be opened for you. There's definitely truth behind the old aphorism, "ya attitude determines ya latitude." With that being said, I'd like to say "keep a positive attitude, spread your wings and fly high."

Pursue Persistently: I can literally write a book on the topic of persistence and how it has propelled those that have chosen to utilize it to achieve tremendous amounts of success. Persistence is definitely one common thread in successful men and women all over the world. We're all familiar with the old saying, "Persistence overcomes resistance." To put it in simple terms, "you persist, persist and keep persisting until you win."

Believe, Believe, Believe. I've just given you the rungs on the ladder of success. The only requirement for them to produce fruit in your life, is to develop a strong belief in them and their capabilities. Another common thread in successful men and women is the unshakable belief in their ability to overcome obstacles and achieve success.

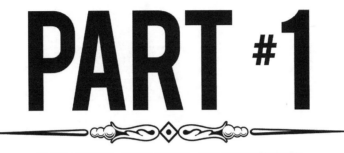

PART #1

"REALITY AND THE AWAKENING"

*"He who rejects change is the architect of decay.
The only human institution which
rejects progress is the cemetery."*
– Harold Wilson

CAS

I first began writing my segment for this book, while I was still incarcerated. I'm sure that may raise the question in some people's minds of "how and why would you write a book about "From D.O.C to C.E.O" if you're incarcerated. The answer to the question is this: Although, I was incarcerated, I didn't have a life sentence; I knew in my heart that upon my release that I was going to advance full speed ahead towards Corporate America. Also, I wanted to write my story of "Incarceration to Incorporation," from the inside to the outside. I've always incorporated different business ventures with the money that I earned from selling drugs, but as a result of selling drugs, I kept ending up incarcerated. For a long period of time, I kept a backwards cycle of "From C.E.O to D.O.C" going (It's supposed to be the other way around obviously). I would sell drugs, take my profits and invest it into some sort of business venture and get locked up shortly afterwards. Then, I would come home and repeat the process, but with the hope of avoiding incarceration. Obviously, things didn't go according to the plan. This is the reason why, after my last arrest, I decided that my crazy cycle of "From C.E.O to D.O.C" had to change. It was time to change my life and correct the dysfunctional cycle and go from "D.O.C to C.E.O." My last arrest occurred on March 4, 2011. I was passing through Reading, PA on my way back from York, PA and was pulled over by the police. After a brief search, the Police discovered 3 pounds of marijuana in my vehicle and from that point, I was arrested and hauled off to prison again. Bail was out of the question, because I was currently on parole at the time form my last drug charge that I had been arrested for in October 2006. I had just gotten released on January 17, 2010 and fourteen months later, I was back in the belly of the beast.

When I was arrested on March 4, 2011, I had two businesses, URBAN LEGENDS BOOKSTORE and URBAN

LEGENDS CLOTHING STORE. I opened the bookstore in July 2010. It was the first black owned bookstore in the history of York, PA. Getting myself arrested, has several people in the community disappointed with me, because not only was it one of its kind in York, Pa, but also it was a great service to the community. Since I didn't have anyone trustworthy to keep the bookstore up and running, it went defunct. This was upsetting to my devoted customers, because before I opened the bookstore, they were traveling to Baltimore, Philadelphia, or online to order books. They hated the idea of going back through that process, especially after I had made things so much better and easier for them.

As I sat inside of my cell at the Reading, Pa County Prison and the initial shock wore off, (98% of most criminals go through the shock phase), and as I accepted reality began to make preparations to fight my case, I could hear the words of Proverbs 20:17 reverberating in my head, "Bread gained by deceit taste sweet to a man, but in the end his mouth shall be filled with gravel." Those words kept playing over and over

4

again in my head. I came to a place in my mind that, it was time to wave the white flag to the street life.

For years, people have been saying to me, "Cas, you're way too intelligent to keep putting it all on line in the streets." "You could be doing so much more." I always appreciated the advice, but at that time, I wasn't ready to quit. The original "AZ" from Harlem, NY released a DVD entitled, "Game Over." Throughout the DVD, he divulges the dark side of "the game" and really gives it up from a real point of view. Towards the end of the DVD, "AZ" goes on to say this about the street life, "The music been stop playing, I don't know why the F*** is people still dancing." I must admit, I felt his words, but I must've heard music playing in my head, because I damn sure still wanted to dance with the streets. Even my good friend since childhood, Author Antoine "Inch" Thomas said something to me one day as I had met up with him to pick up some books for my store. He said, "Cas I now you're doing ya thang on the side in the streets, but ain't nothing worth going back in that cage." I can't express how real those simple words were to me from my childhood friend. However, he had just finished giving the federal penitentiary ten years of his freedom and at that moment in time, he was further along on his journey of change than I was, not to mention, I still wanted to keep hustling to build myself a nice financial nest egg. Sometimes, we'll (myself included) get tunnel vision as we are chasing that paper. We'll only be able to see dollar signs and the reality of all that we risk losing becomes distorted. The point I'm basically trying to make is, sometimes our minds will be so deadlocked on greenbacks, that we'll push the thought of the positive factors to the back of our minds (all the reasons why we shouldn't be doing what we're doing) and it won't be until we get those platinum bracelets on our wrist, that the more intelligent side of us resurfaces. We'll be sitting in a jail cell, kicking ourselves in the behind saying, "Damn, I'm smarter than that." I shouldn't have had to be sitting that cold jail cell to feel the impact of "Inch's" words. Between my religious beliefs, my freedom, my beautiful family, and my two businesses that needed me, I had more than enough reasons to

6

leave the lifestyle behind, but that's where I had to mature in my thinking.

After my last arrest March 4, 2011, I had my ex contact my landlord from my clothing store and ask him if I could break my lease without litigations, due to my circumstances. She informed me that he agreed to let me out of the lease, but she also told me how he cried on the phone. She said he literally began crying on the phone as they were talking, because before I leased the property from him, it had been sitting unoccupied for quite some time. The previous renter had succumbed to cancer. After his unfortunate passing, along with the struggling economy, the landlord had been unable to rent the property until I came along. The Broker that managed the property for the landlord informed me that before they leased me the storefront, there would be a few things that I needed to get done first. Things like transfer the utilities in my name, get renter's insurance on the property, etc, etc. I completed everything the landlord asked me and signed the lease Nov 1, 2010. I developed a great working relationship with the

Landlord and the Broker. Unbeknownst of either of them, I had been selling drugs in the streets. They believed I was just a happy bookstore owner, trying to gradually work my way up the corporate ladder. That's why they were both devastated, when I was arrested a few months later on drug charges. When my ex explained to me that the Landlord cried on the phone to her because I needed to break my lease, I was almost just as hurt for letting my Landlord down, as I was for losing my freedom and my two businesses. That's one of the major reasons why I decided to change. Going back to prison, did not only hurt myself, I hurt a great deal of other people in the process as well. I don't just mean the beautiful five children that the Almighty God blessed me with or my loving family. I mean I hurt people that depended on my business to feed their families as well. People such as the contractors, the painters, the vendors and my employees. The list goes on of people who've come together to help ensure the success of my business. That's why it's very important for us to keep in mind that our actions also affect the lives of others. When I decided

8

that selling drugs and self- destruction was no longer on my list of options, I began my process of self-aggrandizement (education, meditation, studying, career planning, writing, and basically everything conducive to my life's much needed overhaul). I began making preparations for my re-entry into the real world, while I was still incarcerated. I knew life would be harder for me this time around, being that I didn't have drug money as a security blanket, as I had in the past. Truthfully speaking, I felt in my heart that I had something greater in my corner. I had a loving God that patiently waited for me to get my act together, so that he could bless me and any endeavor that I put my hands on.

I started penning my version of Incarceration to Incorporation as I sat in my jail cell, because there wasn't even a shadow of a doubt in my mind that upon my release from prison, I would incorporate. I knew I definitely had a story to tell and a plethora of knowledge to share. I truly believed that my journey could help others look at their life with a new set of eyes and make changes in their own lives. That way, my trial, tribulations, and triumphs didn't only help me grow, but it helped others grow and self-aggrandize. To me, that's a form of giving back, which is something that I am passionate about. In his book entitled "Do You," Russell Simmons said, "If you wanna be successful in life, then help someone else achieve success." That's exactly what I plan to do, by doing everything in my power to help others get their lives back on track.

A few years ago, I met author J.M. Benjamin through my friend Author Antoine "Inch" Thomas, as the Harlem Book Fair. J.M. Benjamin and I communicated periodically afterwards and I had purchased some of his books for my store. As I was sitting in my store one day, I picked up his book entitled, "Incarceration to Incorporation" and began reading it. It turned out to be a really great read, the title and content helped birth the idea of me writing my own story of Incarceration to Incorporation. After all, why not? I was in prison and I got out and incorporated right? I did time and now that I was home, I was incorporated. I was actually sitting behind my counter of the bookstore Incorporated, so why not tell my story. Then, I could've approached J.M. Benjamin about the idea, but the book wouldn't have been sincere, because I was still selling drugs in the streets. Also, in my heart, I know that's being a hypocrite, which is something that I am not. Lastly, I got arrested on this last case eight months after I met J. M. Benjamin. So, the book wouldn't have been available and I wouldn't have been able to do any book signings, while following the necessary steps that it would've taken to help ensure the success of the book. But, the most important thing, as I stated earlier, is that the book wouldn't have been sincere, and to me that isn't cool. I would have gotten no personal fulfillment from that. However, the pages ahead contain my life, my struggles and my triumphs on this journey to entrepreneurship.

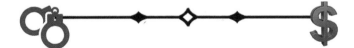

PART #2

"LOCKED DOWN & LOCKED UP"

*"We cannot solve our problems with the same
thinking we used when we created them."*
– Albert Einstein

LOCKED DOWN & LOCKED UP

This topic that I'm about to discuss is probably the most portentous chapter in this book. The reason being is this, if a person decides that they want to change their circumstances in their life, then the first thing that they must do, is change their old way of thinking that caused the circumstances that they're unhappy about.

In order to change, there's a renewing of the mind process that must occur. Without renewing the mind and just hoping for change, is equivalent to a farmer that didn't plant any seeds, but sitting and waiting for a harvest. Author Robert Kiyosaki and Donald Trump released a book years ago called "Why We want You To Be Rich." In one of the chapters they said, "When you make the declaration to be rich, then the poor person inside of you is going to have to die." Basically, in order

14

for the new you to emerge, the old you is going to have to die! It's definitely a mind frame. Which brings us to this chapter.

There's a huge difference between being released from prison and freedom. People are released from prison every day, but that doesn't qualify the individual as being free or having freedom. On the other hand, you have people serving life sentences that'll never walk out of prison, but in their mind, they are as free as the birds gliding through the sky. The difference between the two is this, you have physical bondage and you have mental bondage. There's people walking the streets today and to one looking from the outside, would assume that person is free as a bird. That statement has some truth to a degree. The person may be physically free, but they're locked in a cage mentally. When I was about 18 years old, I came across this cassette tape of Minister Farrahkhan at one of his speaking engagements. Being that it was nearly 20 years ago, since I've listened to it, I don't remember much of the message, however, there was one part of the message that I've never forgotten, "TOO MANY OF US ARE LOCKED

15

DOWN IN THE PRISON SYSTEM AND TOO MANY OF US ARE LOCKED UP IN THE PRISON OF IGNORANCE." Those words alone speak volumes. It's a perfect illustration of physical and mental bondage. Another example of physical and mental bondage comes from the words of the incomparable Jay Z on one of his songs with Oakland, CA's own Too Short, entitled, "A Week Ago." In the song, Jay Z addressed an old friend that broke the code of the streets by snitching to the police. Jay Z told him, "You'll always be in jail, just minus the bars." Jay Z basically tells his former friend that although his body may never step foot inside of a jail cell; mentally he'll be locked in a cell for the rest of his life. Physically trapped in the confines of his guilty conscience.

All situations pertaining to mental incarceration isn't only about snitching. There's numerous ways of being mentally incarcerated. When they opened the front door of S.C.I. Albion for me on February 17, 2009 and told me that I was free to go, I walked into my lady's arms and hugged and kissed her passionately. I got released from state prison, but I was far

16

from free. I knew in my heart that when the time was right, I was definitely going to get me some of that weed money. I got that weed money alright! I got that and a list of other nonsense that came right along with it. I found myself back in state prison, walking the yard with the same select few that I used to walk with before I left. This time, I was saying at least I went out and did what I said that I was going to do. In all reality, that was just justification for coming back to jail. Truth of the matter is, I got off of LOCK DOWN, but I was still LOCKED UP!! It's like, I just went out on a furlough (that hurts me writing it, but it is reality). Whenever a person gets released from prison and goes out there to hustle drugs or gets involved into some form of illegal activity that'll put them right back into the belly of the beast, they're doing what the old timers call, "throwing rocks at the penitentiary," which means you're asking them to let you back inside the prison. Unfortunately, I've thrown a lot of rocks at the penitentiary and they let my behind right back in. I never looked at it like I was deliberately trying to bet back in prison, I just wanted to "do me." I gotta

17

"do me," is a slang term that we love to use in the hood. Most of the time, it's another way of saying, "I'm really putting my life on the line for this money." Doing me needs to be redefined and used in a positive way. Like Russell Simmons best selling novel, entitled, 'Do you." Which gives you the instructions on tapping into your dharma and employing the tools essential for success. When you are fulfilling your purpose in life and helping others along the way, that's when you "Do You."

I've seen dudes walk out of a decent paying job saying, "I'm going to do me and get jammed shortly after. In 2004, I did the same thing. I should've said I'm going to "Do Me In," because that's exactly what I did to myself. I got released from state prison December 12, 2004. Although I was released, I was far from free. Before I got out, the decision to go back to selling drugs had already been made. I had gotten arrested earlier that year, March 2002 (as you can see, by now many of my arrests occurred in the month of March – March 2002, March 2004, March 2011). When I was arrested in March

18

2004, the York City Police wanted me for questioning for a homicide case. My co-defendant from my March 2002 case was being accused of committing the homicide and the York police believed, since he called me after the homicide, that he had informed me about it. I told them that I had absolutely no knowledge whatsoever about the homicide or my old co-defendant. The York City police did not believe me and charged me with hindering apprehension. I sat in the county prison for a few months and the parole board still gave me a parole violation for having a cell phone while on state parole. So after I beat the hindering apprehension charge, my parole officer picked me up and dropped me off at Camp Hill State Prison. At the time of my initial arrest on March 2, 2002, I had a clothing store which had opened a month and a half before my arrest, therefore, another business of mine went down the drain. Finally, the time came for me to be released from state prison. It was about two weeks before Christmas and I had every intention of hitting the streets with a vengeance, getting back everything that I lost and then some. Everything was going as planned until I got set up by a female that I had been dealing with for years. Unbeknownst to me, she had gotten busted by the police and to avoid going to jail, she turned around and set me up. This is a recurring problem around the world. In my younger mind, I would have blamed the girl that set me up, however in my older mature mind, I know that it's "the game" that I owe the blame to. The problem is this, as I stated earlier, when they released me from state prison, I couldn't wait to go and hustle drugs. My way of thinking was all wrong from the start. I shouldn't have walked out of state prison with a vengeance towards the system. If I had to harbor any ill feelings, then, it should've been towards "The Illegal Game" that I loved to play, which allowed the system to take my physical freedom away from me. Many dudes all around the world walk out of the county, state, and federal prison, every day with the vengeance of getting it all back, instead of walking out of prison and being thankful for a second chance at life, because the truth of the matter is this, "you could have died in there!!" It really doesn't matter if the dudes in the jail

20

you were at are built like that or not. Anybody and Everybody is capable of committing a murder. We have to come to a place in our mind that we raise the bar when it comes to our freedom. When you begin to view your freedom as the priceless gift that it is, then you'll be more reluctant about jeopardizing it. It's like the beautiful song by Jill Scott, in which she talks about living her life like its golden. One of the verses she talks about "Taking her freedom off the shelf," which basically means, her freedom is just not up for grabs anymore. Whether she means her physical freedom or mental freedom, it doesn't matter. The bigger picture is that she got her mind in the right place. That's the place in our hearts and minds that we have to come to. The place where our lives and our freedom are precious commodities to us and "the game" is not worth sacrificing our precious commodities.

You'll have to pardon me for making references to a lot of different songs and songwriter's throughout different chapters of this book. It's just that sometimes, we'll hear a song and not really grasp the full meaning of it, or understand

21

the deep message that the songwriter is trying to convey. For instance, Chico Debarge of the Debarge family had a song on his first album that he put out after doing a 6 year bid for dealing drugs. The song was entitled, "The Game." WOW, if you've ever heard the song before, then you already know where I'm at with it. If you've never heard it before, I suggest that you put this book down and go and find the song on iTunes, the internet or wherever you can find it at. In my opinion, no one has ever broke down the effects of the drug game the way Chico Debarge does in this song and he speaks it from experience. If you're incarcerated as you're reading this book and you can't go listen to it, ask your people to go on the internet and find the lyrics to the song and send them to you. Just reading the lyrics to the song will grab you, I promise you on that.

The thing that you must remember is that it's about mental and physical freedom. Once you have the two, you are unstoppable. To attain success and enjoy it, you have to be free. I know a lot of people that are physically free, but they refuse to utilize their God given talents, because locked up in the prison of fear. Fear of what the world might think or simply just the fear of stepping out of their comfort zone. I had a friend that used to make these beautiful mirror clocks. I asked her to make me one for the bookstore, she agreed. People used to come in all of the time and ask about the clock. I mean everyone, from friends, customers and even inspectors. I told her about their interest in the clocks and I also told her that I'd be willing to help her with the start-up money. However, her fear of flying high, outweighed her will to make the clocks a successful business and the idea never came to fruition. Even though my friend served three years in prison for drug dealing and has been walking a straight line ever since her release in 2003, fear had her trapped in the prison of her own mind. She was physically free, but mentally locked up in the prison of her own fear. Another example of mental incarceration is I remember my ex-girlfriend used to say to me, "When you're in jail, I'm doing time also." The ignorant side of me didn't understand that when I was younger, but as I got

23

older, I slowly began to understand the wisdom in her words. By me constantly living a lifestyle that led to prison, it was taking a huge emotional toll on my loved ones. My ex explained that her life was on hold, because I was in prison. She hated making family plans for the family without me being there, or going certain places that we used to go together, that would be painful because I wasn't there with her. Even though we're the ones that endure the physical incarceration, our loved ones suffer from mental incarceration, as a result of us not being there.

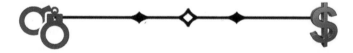

PART #3

"A CHANGED MIND"

"There's nothing as powerful as a changed mind."
— Albert Einstein

A CHANGED MIND

Finally after giving the jail system nearly ten years of my

life, I made the conscious decision that enough was enough. Even

though my ten years of life in the penal system wasn't a straight ten

years, it was completed in increments of one year here, a year and a

half there, nine months here, two and a half years here, and then

another two and a half years. I was doing what many of the lifers

and old timers in prison would call, "The Life Installment Plan."

That's a term for the repeat offender that contributes to the

extremely high recidivism rates. I decided to change and turn my life

around for a number of reasons.

The primary reason is that I always had a feeling in my heart

that God had a special purpose and plan for my life. However, for a

long time, I wasn't ready to follow and commit to that purpose

wholeheartedly. I always felt that I was supposed to be a serial entrepreneur and CEO of a Fortune 500 company, but with my old ways of thinking, I would sell drugs and invest my profits into some business venture; with the hopes of growing that business and never being caught. The problem is that you can't possible believe that you can build a solid foundation on sand. The wind will come and blow that unstable business away and that's exactly what happened to me and my business. How could I think that I was fulfilling my Godly purpose by building my business with drug money? Although some individuals have achieved their businesses and Fortune 500 companies through illegal proceeds, obviously my success was not supposed to be obtained that way. Now I understand, that is why every time that I tried things the wrong way, it fell apart. I would go to jail for dealing drugs and my businesses would go defunct not long after.

The second reason that I decided to change was that I hated the living arrangements of jail that I kept allowing myself to be subjected to. In my old and twisted way of thinking, I kept feeling like they never gave me enough time for the amount of money that I had generated through the years. I know that it's a sick way of looking at things and I humbly thank God that I never received that twenty year sentence, because LORD KNOWS, I was well on my way. Every state has a point system that tabulates all of your arrest convictions, these are used against you at the time of sentencing on new charges. I had been accumulating prior offenses in New York and Pennsylvania, for quite some time. That's why when I was arrested on March 4, 2011, for 3 pounds of marijuana, things got ugly for me real quick. First off, I will say that it's a very sad thing when we find ourselves in ugly situations with people who turn out to be characters others than who we believe them to be. I was arrested with a friend of mine that kept saying, if anything happened, she'll take the charge. Her favorite words day after day were, "What could they do to a white girl with no criminal record."

On March 4, 2011, those words came back and slapped me in the face. Don't get me wrong, as a man, I don't put myself in situations if I can't handle the consequences of my actions. When she and I were arrested on that date, I asked her was she going to take the charge, since she kept saying that she would take one for the team if something ever happened. At the time, she acted as if she would, but told the police behind my back that it wasn't hers. Since she and I were the only ones in the car, everything pointed to me.

Being the real man that I am, I owned up to the marijuana and told them that she had absolutely nothing to do with it and she was exonerated of the charges. If I didn't have a long criminal history of drug offenses, I would have been eligible for probation. For a person without prior offenses, the maximum sentence would only be one year in prison. However, with my priors, the charge carried a minimum sentence of at least two years. I hired a private attorney and explained to him that since I didn't have a lot of positive factors in my corner that would help me win at trial, to go and get me a sensible plea and let me cop out.

On April 15, 2011, I was sentenced and on my way. Some of my friends said that I should've kept fighting, maybe things would've gotten better. Truthfully speaking, the game and all of the bullshit that comes with it had taken its toll on me. I didn't feel like fighting and playing with them people any longer. I was honestly tired. Many people only complain when they get caught. That, truly wasn't the case with me. I was getting tired of it before I was caught. The money was coming in good, but the paranoia was wearing me thin. I always have been a strategic type of hustler and trying to outthink the police, snitches, and my parole officer was getting to me.

Therefore, when I arrested on March 4, 2011, I said enough is enough. I made the decision that I would never hustle drugs again. It was time for me to build my brand and build it on a firm and solid foundation.

On my previous bids, I had written six movie scripts and when I went home the last time, I incorporated WINDOE FILMS, with my childhood friend and comrade Jamie-O, but the company didn't stand a chance. Shortly after we incorporated, he went to jail on drug charges. Three weeks after his release, I was arrested on drug charges. As I sat in my cell, all that I thought about was how I was losing two stores and WINDOE FILMS, as well as how they would be inactive for the next few years. The game allowed myself and my business partner Jamie-O to get entangled in the web of a vicious cycle. I came to realize that I was losing everything that I had gained, and I didn't want to play that game any longer.

I remember calling home and speaking to my ex-girlfriend before we broke up and telling her that I was finally done with the street life. It felt as if I could see her smiling through the telephone. She was elated because for a number of years she endured a long turbulent road with me living life as a drug dealer. Her and I first got together in October 2003. We had both just finished doing time in the penitentiary and were in halfway houses. I didn't know her prior to us going to prison, but we were both employed through the same temp agency. We both were working at Stauffers Biscuit Company, which is where we met. We immediately both feel head over heels for each other. The only problem was that she no longer wanted anything to do with the street life and me on the other hand was waiting for the right moment to dive right back into the game. I knew that once they let me out of the halfway house, that it was on. When that time came and I got my package, I called and said, "Baby, I gotta go handle some business." Her reply was, "What do you mean, some business, we don't go to work until 11 o'clock." As soon as I explained to her what I meant, I could hear her crying through the phone. Then she told me that we were going to have to go our separate ways. I immediately drove and picked her up from her mother's house and took her out to a restaurant so that we could talk things over. I was in love and I didn't want to lose her. I explained to her that I wasn't trying to make a career out of it, (which is something that everybody says) and that I only wanted to open my clothing store and stack enough money to go into film production.

She compromised her beliefs and decided to stay with me. A few months went by and early in 2004, she was there as I got the clothing store. Things were looking good, but as always with the game, things took a turn for the worse. I was arrested on March 2, 2004 and everything went down the drain. She supported me through the entire ordeal, even though she never wanted to go through the process of being a prisoner's wife again. When I was released on December 13, 2004, she was there to pick me up. She prayed that I was done with the street life, but I wasn't, I jumped right back in. I was arrested again on October 6, 2006 after being set up by a so called friend. I got out on bail and 10 months later, I was sentenced to 2 ½ - 5 years in state prison. This time, she was pregnant with our second child. At my sentencing, I was remanded by the judge to begin serving my time immediately. My pregnant girlfriend was in the courtroom crying her eyes out. However, once again, she gave me her unwavering love and support throughout my bid. When I came home, I found myself again asking her not to leave me, because I wasn't ready to give up hustling in the streets. Once again, I convinced her to stay with me and that I was only going to do it to get my businesses up and running. Many, Many, hustlers say that same thing, "I just want to do it until I get this or that," but somewhere on their way to achieving that goal, they either lose themselves in the process or go to jail. Some actually achieve the goal they set, but they don't stop there. They end up setting higher goals and repeat the process until they crash and burn, myself included.

After doing my 2 ½ - 5 years, I jumped right back into it and things went extremely well for quite some time. I had two businesses and I began buying equipment for my film production company, WINDOE FILMS. However, on March 4, 2011, I got busted again and it all fell apart. Being my own worst critic, I had an honest talk with myself and I came to the realization that trying to build my business with drug money, obviously wasn't going to happen. That's why after my last arrest on March 4, 2011, I had reached my breaking point. That is why, when I called her one day from the county prison and told her that I was finally giving up hustling in the streets, she was elated beyond comprehension. She knew that I had said it from a sincere heart, because I've never been one of them dudes in jail that just says things because of the situation that they're in, then come home and do something different. I always made it my business to be real with myself. If I wanted to come home and sell drugs, then that's exactly what I would do.

So, when I informed her that I was done, she smiled from the inside out. Her being someone whom I spent years in a close relationship, she knew me like the back of my hand. She knew whatever I put my mind to, I wouldn't stop until my goal was achieved.

Now, with me refocused on rebuilding my businesses the right way, nothing can stop me. Unfortunately, my relationship with my girlfriend didn't withstand the test of time. She reached the point, where she continued to offer support as a friend and as the mother of my youngest children. She had reached her breaking point, which was totally understandable. Ever since I was a kid, I've always used setbacks, disappointments, and heartache as motivation to keep going. My beautiful mother told me a long time ago that, "Everything in life is a lesson or a blessing. Some situations are both." That's why whenever I'm faced with disappointment or hardship, I think about those words from my mother and keep pushing forward. Make no mistake about it, it's not always an easy thing to do, but we must do what we have to do. My motto for my film company, WINDOE FILMS, is that "great art comes from great pain." I am a firm believer of that motto and that's why when my girlfriend and I parted ways, I took a long look at the man in the mirror. I realized it was time to get right as a whole. I restored my relationship with Almighty God first and by reorganized my priorities, which is how I came up with the TeamSuccess paradigm. Some of the wonderful work from the late Tupac Shakur was written in his cell at Clinton Correctional Facility. Some of his greatest songs were conceived in his jail cell, as he probably had a lot of disappointment on his plate. Writing became a catharsis for him. GREAT ART CAME FROM GREAT PAIN.

I've been a vicarious reader of business and self -help books. I also love to watch TV shows that give me pointers and invaluable information that could help make me a better entrepreneur. In prison, I absolutely made it my business every Friday night to watch Shark Tank. If you're not familiar with the show, it's a show where fledging entrepreneurs go in front of a panel of investors and give a bio of their business in the hopes of getting one of the wealthy panelists to invest in their company. Damon John of FUBU is one of the panelist that will invest his hard earned money, if the right opportunity presents itself. On one particular episode, Damon said, "Life is 20% of what happens to you and 80% of how you respond to it." I can't even begin to explain to you how much those words mirrored my feelings. I strongly felt like, even though I had been through a lot of bullshit, and made mistakes along the way, it would be my finish that would help to inspire others. That's why I began writing this book, because me getting arrested and losing two businesses, along with losing some other things, would represent the 20% and me going home, incorporating the TeamSuccess Publications L.L.C, along with rebuilding my businesses the right way, would represent the 80%.

I always believed that I could be doing so much more on a larger positive scale, than what I was doing in the streets. Don't get me wrong, it ain't like I'm saying that I was a 8 ball hustler that could've done better by working at McDonald's. I'm not saying that to dis any of the 8 ball hustlers or the kid working at McDonald's, but by the age of 18, I was considered "Hood Rich." I just had a strong gut feelings that I should be in corporate America, really doing my thing. It's like, when Jay-Z said, "I could make 40 off a brick/but one rhyme could beat that." That is the case with a lot of us. On my last bid, I started writing a book called, "The Hip Hop Guide To Healing The Criminal Heart." Throughout the book, I spoke about how through the years, I've met dudes in jail that were so talented, but they never put it to good use. Many are trapped in the mind frame of thinking that because they've been to prison, it's over for them. I explain throughout the book, that it's never over, unless you want it to be over.

Basically, I want the reader to understand, that the only thing that'll stop them is their own way of thinking. I speak about people that were incarcerated and went home and made it happen. People need to understand that Brian "Baby" Williams of Cash Money Records went to prison and look at what he's achieved since his release. Lyfe Jennings, Vickie Stringer served years in prison and came home and built a publishing empire, and the list goes on. We can't use prison as an excuse not to achieve. Obviously, there'll be occupations a convicted felon need not to pursue, like President of the United States of America. The similarity between the successful and the unsuccessful is this, we all have only 24 hours in a day, but what differentiates the two is how each one uses their twenty four. The successful utilize their time on activities conducive to empowerment. (This is not only about material wealth). The world can be your playground, if you utilize the principles necessary for success and believe it without wavering. Things will work out for you, myself included. I'm a huge fan of Tyler Perry and the work that he has put in to get where he is at today. His company, Tyler Perry Studios, is an entertainment powerhouse. Tyler Perry was once incarcerated as well, It may not have been for a long period of time, however, he was there as well and was homeless for quite some time. But, it's the way that he turned his misfortunes into fortunes, which tells a lot about his character. I always have had a strong feeling in my heart that I could be a huge asset to the world. I just struggled for a long time constantly trying to make my dreams materialize with profits from drug money. But that way of thinking only led me to prison and my business ventures went down the drain in the process. In 2000, I started my own clothing line. As with any business, you'll have your ups and downs. At one point, I decided to step away from hustling for a little while and focus on my clothing line Cashmere Clothing Company. Everyone in New York and other states called me by the nickname Casper, except for my O.G. friend, Dezoe. Before the feds snatched Dezoe in 1993, he never liked calling me

Casper, because he felt like the name was hot. He said that I was a smooth money getter and he gave me the name Cashmere. The feds snatched Dezoe a short time later and he was sentenced to 300 months. I can't even explain how hurt I was when he got snatched and was sentenced. He honestly was a big brother and friend to me. He gave me a lot of knowledge before he was taken away. That's why when I started the clothing line, I called it Cashmere Clothing Company.

I always felt in my heart that in the process of the federal government taking his freedom away, he helped me change my life and my way of thinking for the better. Cashmere would represent the more intelligent side of me. Even though starting the clothing line was one of my brightest ideas to this date, I made a lot, and I mean a lot of mistakes. It wasn't like I went to school to learn anything about designing clothes. I had no experience or knowledge about the fashion industry. I just came up with the idea and took my drug money and jumped right in. I began to create a nice buzz in New York City and a few other states. Building a business requires knowledge, sacrifice and wise counsel, along with some other business principles that'll help you achieve success. I had absolutely none of the above. To make matters worse, I had some negative people around me that would give me nothing but bad advice. I had orders from 15 stores for Cashmere T-Shirts, but I was running low on money and with the advice from one of my so called friends, I resorted back to selling drugs in Pennsylvania. Less than 6 months that same friend and I were locked down in York County Prison on drug possession charges. I had orders from 15 stores and I thought running around selling and transporting drugs was more important, instead of figuring out a positive way to fulfill the orders. I went back to what I knew best, which was selling drugs and not long after, I was in prison thinking about those 15 stores that placed orders with and I would be letting them down. But even then, after feeling and looking stupid in the face because I let the stores down and sacrificed my freedom in the process, I still had a tremendous amount of growing up mentally to do. That's why I would end up going on to do 3 more state bids after that one.

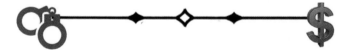

PART #4

"RELEASE AND RESURGENCE"

"There are no shortcuts to any place worth going."
— Beverly Sills

RELEASE AND RESURGENCE

On September 9, 2013, I walked out of Albion State Penitentiary eager to regain my freedom and lead my team to victory. My mother who was my biggest supporter, my sister Shanita, and my cousin Zaria were all patiently waiting for me at the front gate.

After being arrested for three pounds of marijuana, losing two businesses and serving nearly three years in prison, I was finally released and the moment was surreal. I came home with ginormous plans of making my name well known in the real estate industry and doing my thing in Corporate America. Although I made some invaluable connections days after my release and was quickly familiarizing myself with the real estate market I lived in. The shock of finally being home still loomed over me and lasted about three weeks. Upon my release from

Prison, my zest for success far outweighed my financial stability, therefore, I had no idea of some of the challenges, pitfalls, and heartaches that all awaited me on my journey to success. Before I was released from prison, I studied real estate investing for at least 5 – 9 hours a day, 5 days a week. That lasted from the beginning of my bid until the very end. I totally immersed myself in my studies. Since I knew that my credit wasn't the greatest and that I wasn't coming home to a lot of money, I search diligently for the best source to acquire properties for pennies on the dollar. I really needed to find out how I could purchase properties for the lowest amount possible. I was so overzealous that not only was I not concerned about how bad of a condition that the property would be in, but also I was totally willing to disregard the three "most important" words in real estate, which are location, location, location. I felt like if I found a property at an affordable price point, or the seller was willing to finance his property to me under favorable terms, that I didn't care if the property was in deplorable conditions or if it was in the worst neighborhood. After learning about tax liens, sheriff sales, and the Redevelopment Authority, I couldn't wait to get home so that I could approach their offices and make my presence felt. Three days after my release, I made my way to the office of the Redevelopment Authority of York and as fate would have it, as I entered the office, the Director of Economic Development was walking by and politely asked me, "How can I help you?" Me being the brutally honest individual that I am, I laid it out on the table. When I say brutally honest, I mean exactly that. I went into how I initially came down from New York to hustle drugs and had various businesses and how I had just gotten released from State Prison and was in a halfway house. By the grace of God, he actually took a liking to me and felt my energy and from that moment a business/friendship relationship was formed. I learned that purchasing from the Redevelopment Authority wasn't as easy as I had perceived it to be. It was true that I could purchase properties from them at a steep discount, but what I was completely unprepared for was the strict criterion that was in place in order for one to be purchased

44

from them. It was much more of a complex transaction that just having the capital on hand, and them selling the properties, and both parties walking away after the deed is transferred. Most of the properties from the Redevelopment Authority require some renovations, and before the property can be sold to you, they want to ascertain that you have the where withal to make it habitable in a timely fashion, not to mention, everything must be done according to code. It was an arduous process that I wasn't ready for at that moment, especially just after being released from prison. However, under the tutelage of some seasoned real estate investors, I went back to the drawing board and professionalized my business. I did a name availability search and once I receive approval from the PA Department of Sate to use the name, I actually incorporated Blight Doctor Properties, LLC. I chose that name because in my previous lifestyle, it was men like myself that destroyed the community by selling drugs and committing acts of violence. Therefore, once I turned my life around and made the decision to invest in real estate, I told myself that it is only right that I take a proactive role in the construction of many of the communities that I personally had a role in the destruction of.

When I initially found out about the complicated process of the Redevelopment Authority and all of the prerequisites that must be submitted in the proposal in order to purchase from them, I started approaching various organizations that are listed as advocates in community development and explained to them who I was, my plan to combat blight and for their assistance. They all stated that they loved my plan, but since the company wasn't a not – for – profit organization, that they couldn't help me. I must honestly admit the rejection hurt a little bit, but after thinking things through, I realized that the rejection did more good than bad in many ways. It enabled me to weed out the unfruitful seeds and focus on the beneficial ones. I knew that I would do what I had to regardless of whatever opposition I had encountered. Primarily, my reason for going to those organizations was so that I could find the people that were offering help to individuals in my community. This way, whenever I consult

46

with men and women that sincerely want to change, but feel hindered by their criminal background, I can point them in the direction of the resources at their disposal. My overall mission is and always will be to help others. I didn't mind being turned away after applying for various grants and loans. I was willing to persist until I found the one particular organization that said, "yes." This way, whenever I have one of my counseling sessions with a man/woman, I could guide them through the process of purchasing blighted properties at affordable prices and point them in the director of rehabilitation money, if needed. By no means am I saying that it is an easy and simple process, but it's definitely worth it and it's an outlet that if done correctly, it could provide substantial income so that one doesn't have to resort back to their old ways.

Even though my real estate company is still fairly new, we have an extremely great future ahead of us. I will be releasing a real estate book through my TeamSuccess Publications Company, entitled, "From Selling Kilos, To Selling Condos." It will be an in depth book explaining my journey from the street life, to investing in the world's second oldest profession. The book will definitely divulge everything that transpired between me going from one hustle to the next. I truly believe it's a good book and expect for it to be helpful to anyone interested in getting started in the real estate business. Although real estate is a business that I'm extremely passionate about, it is not my only business venture.

Now, my bookstore, the infamous Urban Legends Bookstore is and always will be one of my investment babies. There's an old saying, "Anything that's worth having is worth fighting for." There definitely must be some truth behind that old aphorism, because since my release from prison, I've encountered problem after problem trying to get to the finish line and reopen my bookstore. One of the things that I'm happy about is that I have over fifteen years of studying the habits and psychology of successful people. Therefore, whenever I reach a fork in the road, I can recall and ponder on the struggles they faced and the methods that they employed to overcome their struggles and use that as motivation for myself.

I remember having to ponder the wisdom of the late John H. Johnson to help me push forward as he described the struggle on his journey to success. He said, "Whenever I hit a barrier in the road, I curse, I cry and then I get a ladder and climb right over it. The wisdom of Mr. Johnson's words certainly served as inspiration to keep going when I encountered obstacles. The first barrier that I hit on my path to reopening Urban Legends came about one week after my release from State Prison. I went to my storage unit for the first time in three years to check on my belongings from the bookstore. I went there under the belief that I had over four thousand books still left in my inventory, because prior to going to jail I was stockpiling my inventory. I figured that I would only need to purchase all of the new books and sequels that were released in the three years of my absence. I opened my storage unit and to my dismay, all of my books were gone. I was shocked beyond comprehension. The locks weren't broken into or anything. It obviously was an inside job. I found out who the culprit was and that was my first major test after being home for only a few

49

days. What an awkward position I found myself in. Now, as I look back in retrospect, I believe it was a test of my mental and spiritual growth. I had just left the State Penitentiary where I had friends who were literally sentenced to death behind those prison walls and would never have the opportunity to spend a day with their loved ones in the free world ever again. I had a serious decision to make, was I going to resort to my old ways and end up just like one of my lifer friends, or was I going to let it go and stay focused on rebuilding my entrepreneurial endeavors righteously. I knew good and well that me being the blessed go – getter that I am, that I would certainly get it all back tenfold as long as I remained free. Truthfully speaking, my pride and ego were more hurt than the actual loss of the books. Pride and ego are definitely two deadly pills to swallow that have destroyed many men upon consumption. Thank God, I'd been on earth long enough to know that there are way too many men serving life sentences or are in the graveyard as a result of making irrational decisions based on pride and ego. Needless to say, I sucked it up and took the loss. The man that

I am today can honestly say that I'm extremely happy that I did because I didn't jeopardize my freedom and now I have multiple streams of income being generated simultaneously. I'd be lying to you if I sad that the decision to let it go was easy, because it wasn't. That's why I strongly believe that we must always remain spiritually grounded, because otherwise we'll give the devil (inner destroyer) too much unneeded leverage to come in and destroy all that we've worked too hard to build. I heard a voice in my head saying, "The worst thing a winner could do, is to throw it all away for a loser." I know that was the voice of the Almighty God. I'm elated beyond comprehension that I listened to my inner creator. As I stayed focused and kept pressing towards achieving my goals legally, doors were opening for me. I had finally gotten my first storefront after being home for nearly a year. It wasn't in that great of a location as my previous bookstore, but nonetheless, it was still located in a high-traffic area. The store needed some renovations and I worked diligently to get them done while simultaneously going to work at my regular job, college and handling various tasks for my real estate company. It was extremely strenuous on me physically and financially, trying to balance it all out, but by the Grace of Almighty God, I made a tremendous amount of progress. I completed all of the major renovations (not me personally, but through the contractor) and began hanging my shelves up along with all of my pictures that I had taken with numerous Authors in the literary industry. Although I wasn't completely at the finish line, it felt good putting my key in the door and seeing the progress that was made. I was elated at the fact that my goal of reopening my bookstore was coming to fruition and I wasn't compromising my freedom as a result of doing so.

As I was feeling overjoyed at the way it was all coming together, I didn't have the slightest clue of the next turn of events that would not only be extremely hurtful to me, but would test me in such a way where I had to stop and evaluate which was more important to me, success or failure. Without delving into too much details for obvious legal reasons, I was betrayed by someone whom I held near and dear to my heart. I caught the person hanging out with the culprit who had stolen my books. The person had promised me that they had severed all ties and communication with the culprit after my books were stolen. I'd be lying if I said I wasn't hurt behind the situation, but my spirit just kept telling me to stay focused and keep pushing in the direction of my purpose. It was definitely one of the moments where I learned that I was really at a place where succeeding meant more to me than failing because the old me would've handled things differently. But nonetheless, God is in the redemption business and he changed me. With that being said, I knew I had to sever some ties, pick up the pieces and keep striving. Part of the moving on process required that I move out of my home, but another major problem came as I assess my financial capabilities. I had to ask myself, how was I going to pay all of the bills at my new place, still give my children's mother the cash outlays that I give her on a monthly basis for our children and still pay all the bills at my store. My real estate company was struggling, so I couldn't count on it to help with the situation, and I had squandered the bulk of my savings on the renovations that were done to my store. The truth of the matter was this, based on the income from my job, it wasn't enough money coming in to pay for all of the outgoing expenses. Unfortunately, my store had to be the sacrifice. It was tough, but I had to prioritize. The amazing thing about divine design, is that as a result of me staying focused and continuing to live righteously despite the obstacles and hardships, doors continued opening for me. Another blessing came through a few months later, I received a call from my good friend/business partner Wynn Kearse that the storefront adjacent to his business had just become available and was being offered for below market value. The space was double the size that I had just lost and was being offered for the same amount of money. The new space did need renovations as the previous space did, but overall it was still a blessing.

Upon my release from prison, I started listening to some highly-notable motivational speakers and began fostering relationships with some of them. Another one of the things

54

that I'm happy about is the fact that they opened my mind to different ways of giving back and social contributions. As a result, I didn't want to just open another bookstore. This time around, I developed a larger vision of my bookstore. I wanted to do something empowering for the youth. I made the decision that I would reopen as a bookstore/learning center and the bigger space afforded me the ideal location to do so. I ended up having to go through an arduous legal battle over zoning issues, because of the stores location and York City ordinance regulations. However, in the end, by the grace of Almighty God, favorable results followed. My bookstore will soon be reopened and I'm elated beyond comprehension.

The lesson that I learned from this whole ordeal as I work diligently to get to the finish line is this, anything that's worth having is definitely worth persevering through all of the barriers and setbacks that you encountered along the way. Sometimes the character traits that you develop along the journey is better than the financial prize you receive in the end. My bookstore means a lot to me. When I first opened it back in 2011, people frequently asked me why would I open a bookstore at a time when not only mom and pop bookstores were closing, but even the larger recognized bookstores were either struggling to keep their doors open or they were outright shutting down. My answer to the questions would always be the same, because reading is my passion and readers are leaders. I concur with billionaire businessman Kevin O'Leary's theory of "follow your passion and you'll get rich without even noticing it." I knew it was a risky move opening a bookstore in such a volatile market, but when it comes to my businesses, I strongly believe in devising winning strategies rather than just focusing on not losing. I say that, because there's a difference between winning and not losing. It's a different mindset. The bookstore did pretty fair numbers prior to me going to prison, and now anticipation from my beloved supporters, I expect to do even greater numbers. People know books, reading and education is something that I am extremely passionate about. Therefore, they know that I will always work diligently to keep my shelves stocked with hard to find material, with the built up classics and the newest highly sought after literature. Now don't get me wrong, I am extremely appreciative of the financial support that we get from the community. However, I went into this investment under the mindset of contributing to the common good of the people first and hoping that the profits would follow shortly thereafter. I strongly believe in the immeasurable power of a book. That's why I'm elated whenever someone purchases a book from me, because I know that there's some information contained within the pages that could literally change a person's perception on life. That perception could be the starting point of tremendous improvement for that individual. That's the kind of service that fuels my entrepreneurial fire. If there's anything that I want people, especially that person that is soon to be released or just came home from prison, is that yes, it was tough getting a simple bookstore reopened, but I did it and you can too. You just have to decide what it is that you really want to do and be willing to go the distance, display the tenacity in the face of adversity, and keep doing so until you win. I say that because, it was definitely a battle for me. I made it happen off of a ten dollar an hour job. Now, the reality of life is this, I had to pay taxes, child support and bills first and foremost. From that point, whatever was left, I used to invest. I got small things done week after week and that's the mentality that I would like for others to adopt as they venture into business ownership. Don't stress yourself out worrying about getting big things done. Keep doing little things and do them well. It wasn't easy for me, but nonetheless, I made it happen and you can too. I embraced the struggle, because it is imperative to me to help men and women coming home from the Department of Corrections know that they are capable of starting their own business as well. It can be done without jeopardizing his/her freedom. However, if I made it sound simple or easy, please allow me to eradicate any misconceptions. Unless you have some huge nest egg, investors, or excellent credit, getting start-up capital is an arduous process and it can be frustrating, but you have to keep in mind that the mission is not impossible. Things may not happen in the timely fashion that you would like, but know that running a little behind inside the race is much better than watching from the sidelines. This has been a two year process for me. Prior to my release, I would've bet my left arm that I would've had my store re-opened within 3-6 months after my release. Unfortunately, events occurred and situations happened that temporarily derailed my progress. In my heart, I knew that the Almighty God made me stronger than the knockdown. That's what I want you, the reader to understand. Life will hit you hard, but you have to utilize your inherent resilience, get back on track, and persist until you achieve your goal. I, Jemell Hill, totally concur with Black Enterprise Magazine and their declaration of financial empowerment, where they said, "We should maximize our earning power." It is our inalienable right to create multiple streams of income if we choose to. I know that's another one of those things that's easier said than done, but it should ultimately be your goal and one that you work diligently towards. Another company that I incorporated is TeamSuccess Publications, LLC, which is my own book publishing company.

I know that I could've went after a traditional book deal with one of the many publishing houses that I'm in contact with, because of my bookstore, but traditional publishing deals could be a time consuming process coupled with a myriad of paperwork. I chose not to go that route for a number of reasons. The first and foremost reason is that I'm not that trusting in a company's capability of hustling for my project as hard as I would. There's not a shadow of a doubt in my mind that if my success or failure is predicated on my ability or inability to hustle, that I would work ceaselessly until I succeeded at whatever the goal was. I've always had the innate tendency to go hard at whatever I did regardless if it was good or bad. At the time of this writing, I was at a place in my life where I needed a game changer, and in my heart of hearts, I felt that self-publishing would be the game changer I needed.

My book, "From D.O.C. to C.E.O." is the first release from my TeamSuccess Publishing Company and I have every intention of getting this book in the hands of readers all around the world. It is a dire mission of mine to convey my story to men and women across the globe that businesses can be started, dreams can come to fruition, and reasonable goals can be achieved righteously. You just have to make a declaration that no matter what difficulties or setbacks you encounter along the way, you learn from them, overcome them and keep pushing forward. D.O.C. to C.E.O is the first of a series of books to be released from TeamSuccess Publications. I released this book first because it really weighs on my heart to help people like myself that were in the streets look at life from a different perspective and embrace the reality that it is possible to live a successful life without compromising your freedom. This is such a serious thing for me, because I know from experience how the street life is destroying people. I was one of those people. It put massive amounts of money in my pockets, but the destruction far outweighed the finances. In the end, it's never worth it. That's what I want people to understand. Refocus and get this money the right way. That's the purpose of this book. The second release from TeamSuccess Publications will be the highly anticipated book I wrote entitled, "#TeamSuccess." It is definitely a great book that I'm extremely excited about. I envision the book having a profound effect on the world in general. I visualize the #TeamSuccess book helping to strengthen marriages, parent and children relationships, friendships, businesses, and just serving as an overall guide to empowerment. Whenever I do a speaking engagement and I break down my whole empowerment theory of Team Success, it enamors me to see the joy on the listeners faces as they grasp the concept and visualize incorporating it into their own lives. Most of the time when I stop and share it with someone, they are well pleased with the idea of the entire concept. Basically, because of how well my TeamSuccess way of thinking is working in my life and the lives of people that are close to me, I was compelled to write a book about it and share it with the world. Please stay tuned and keep your eye out for that book and hopefully it'll help change your life in a wonderful way. As I stated earlier in this chapter, I will also be releasing a real estate book through this company and it should be helpful to anyone with even a modicum of interest in the real estate business. As the company grows, I look to being in a position to sign other authors and give them the opportunity to showcase their talent to the world. Please stay locked in and in tune with us at TeamSuccess and know that I will be working diligently to bring you really good educational and entertaining literature.

Well my peoples, I've reached that point where it's now time for me to bring this book to an end. But before I end, let me make another attempt to eradicate any misconceptions that one may have about my journey from D.O.C. to C.E.O. There are three sets of circumstances that can be a grueling and arduous process and I endured all three patiently, faithfully, and tenaciously. They are:

(1)   Being confined to a prison cell

(2)   Changing your life around (this is tough for people like myself. Most of the time we'd rather take our chances by resorting back to what we know best, rather than embracing the unfamiliarity. We would take the risk despite the harsh penalties that we know awaits us if we get caught.)

(3)   Starting and running a business

With that being said, please know that my journey from D.O.C. has been a long and laborious road. I sat in my jail cell with a vision and upon my release, I walked out of state prison and made a declaration to myself that no matter what obstacles, heartaches, or setbacks I encountered, I would remain committed to change and would rebuild my businesses within the parameters of the law. Of course there were times when my declaration was tested when life had its' way of knocking me down, however, I simply reminded myself that trials and tribulations were a part of the process in order to receive the prize. That way of thinking is what reinvigorated me to pick up the pieces and persevere with assurance that the mission was not impossible. By the grace of God, I persisted until I incorporated and the man I am today is a legitimate business owner, entrepreneur, motivational speaker, and most importantly a child of the Almighty God that looks forward to inspiring and helping others understand that they too can go from the "D.O.C. to C.E.O." without having to compromise or sacrifice this golden gift that we all call freedom.

FROM DEPARTMENT OF CORRECTIONS

TO

CHIEF EXECUTIVE OFFICER

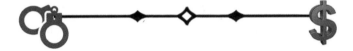

PREVENTION
BEFORE
INTERVENTION

"A MESSAGE TO THE SCHOOL SYSTEM"

*"It is easier to build strong children than
to repair broken men."*
– Frederick Douglass

A MESSAGE TO THE SCHOOL SYSTEM

When my good friend Jamiel Alexander first suggested to me that I should have a chapter geared specifically towards the youth in our school system, at first it didn't dawn on me how important it was for me to reach our young men and women. I was so deadlocked on doing my part and trying to help men and women like myself whom destroyed a good number of years of their lives, that I hadn't really dedicated any portion of my book to the youth, our future leaders. So after we discussed it further and I thought about it afterwards, it not only made perfect sense, but it was a priority that needed to be addressed immediately. I started doing some research and came across some really saddening information. I learned that people are saying that schools in the urban communities are now becoming a pipeline to the prison system. That's extremely saddening because that's not what our school system was designed for. Even in impoverished neighborhoods, schools are supposed to be one of the pipelines to help our youth become productive members of society. Now I'm not placing the burden solely on the school system, I agree with the old adage that it takes a village to raise a child, which is why I strongly believe that collectively (parents, teachers, and members of the community), have to work together to do everything in our power to deter our youth from choosing the "street dream." Which will only have them awakened to the harsh reality of jail, death, and destruction.

One of the sad and threatening dangers of this day and age is that the whole "street drug dealer image" has evolved into a culture. That is extremely dangerous for our youth, because cultures usually come with the "cool factor" and "cool factors" have a way of alluring people in. The last thing that we need is for more of our young men and women being allured into a lifestyle of heartache and ruin. That poses a major

69

problem for all of us. I say us, because our youth represent a reflection of the direction of our future. When I was selling drugs, even though I never verbally expressed it out of my mouth to the youth that selling drugs was cool, I know inadvertently, I may have gave them the impression through my flamboyant lifestyle. Therefore, I will take a proactive role in teaching our youth that the street lifestyle isn't the glamorous, easy, and praiseworthy lifestyle that it's falsely perceived to be. I've met way too many men all around the world whom like myself got involved in the streets at an early age and have wasted so many good years of our lives being in the opposite direction of our purpose. I can honestly say from personal experience, that even though I may have had the accouterments of success, that I was far from successful. I was extremely paranoid and the end result was me being incarcerated. The street life shouldn't even be referenced as a game, because it has absolutely no winners. We have to do everything in our power to discourage our youth from entering that game of destruction and encourage them to focus their thoughts on living a lifestyle of righteousness and construction.

I do believe that it's men like myself that have invaluable information to impart with the youth in our school system, because I know every aspect of that lifestyle and everything that it has to offer. I can also speak on the wonderful benefits of achieving their goals honestly. In most neighborhoods of the inner cities, children look up to the drug dealers with the highly desired material possessions without truly understanding that the price tag (jail, death, betrayal, pain) for material possessions far exceed their worth. That's why we have to teach our youth about the alternatives. It's imperative that they understand that success is highly possible without compromising their lives or their freedom, as well as they don't have to lose any cool points in the process. Speaking of cool points, I strongly believe that one of the ways to save or disentangle our adolescents is to help redefine some of the things that they consider being cool. I've personally seen certain tragic events happen and people perceived it as cool. For example, I knew an individual that had shot numerous people on different occasions and there were people that looked at the individual with admiration because of the distorted values and beliefs that our youth are being taught today. Shooting someone is never a glorious or cool thing, not even in self-defense situations. Another sad thing that is perceived as cool in "the hood," is the longer a person does in prison, the more cool points he receives in "the hood." This distorted viewpoint gives our youth the perception that going to prison is cool and it also makes them believe that it's the way to receive credibility in their neighborhood. I personally have friends that have served over 20 years in prison and seen how upon their release people praised them, as if they had just come back from college. Now don't get me wrong, I'm happy to see people get released from incarceration, but let's not glorify the activities that lead to lengthy prison sentences. I totally understand that the loss of freedom can be devastating to the particular individual that loses it and it can also be devastating to the person's family, so I definitely understand the desire to celebrate upon that individual's release. All that I am saying, is that we have to be extra careful to not convey the wrong message to the children.

As I stated earlier, one of the ways we'll be effective in our children's lives, is by redefining many of the values and activities that our youth think are cool. Our young generation needs to know and understand that there's absolutely no glory to be gained by going to prison regardless of what they may see and hear in music or in the streets. We have to come together and help break the mental generational curses that have been passed on to our young children and reposition them for future success. I strongly believe that it is my responsibility to inform young men and women of the dangers and pitfalls of the streets and all they may appear to have to offer. Through my books and my teachings, it is my wish to save the younger generation from years of detainment, inertia and all the disappointments that follow as a result of living a life of crime. It's imperative for our youth to understand that they were all born with an innate gift that once it's nurtured and developed, they can be of great service to the world. Between people like myself, parents,

73

the school system, and other community members all working together in unison in our children's lives, it puts us at a huge vantage point in helping our youth become the Attorney's, Neurologists, Meteorologists, Bankers, and people in notable positions in life as they were purposely willed to be. The onus is on us to help them see their unlimited capabilities despite what they may see taking place in their neighborhoods.

As I bring this section to an end, hopefully this will be the beginning of a powerful union that will work together on one accord towards the empowerment of our young leaders. The title of this particular section is "Prevention before Intervention," because we need to reach our children before the Judge slams down his gavel and sentences them, or the Coroner makes that unfortunate call to their parents. It is of the utmost importance that we work diligently to keep our adolescents far from the clutches of the virulent streets and focused on living the meaningful and fulfilled lives that they were divinely designed to live.

My name is Jemell Jarod Hill and my company is called

TeamSuccess, which is why I repeatedly use words like us, we, and together, because by working together it greatly increases our chances of producing highly favorable results. I sincerely look forward to us collaborating and making a significant difference in the lives of our future leaders. Until then, I will continue to be an active advocate for the empowerment of our youth. I am a firm believer of the old adage: Inspire the gifts of each individual and the team will succeed.

Sincerely,

Jemell Hill

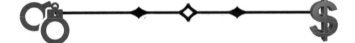

FROM ONE HUSTLER TO ANOTHER

From one hustler to another, it's definitely time to flip the page. Keeping it all the way honest, the streets are just plain bad news. Forget me using the big words and eloquent speaking. We're just going to call it like it is, the whole state of "The Game." Right now, it is outright ugly. As I was writing this, a good friend of mine just got sentenced to 18 years in prison for possession of four ounces of crack cocaine and he had just gotten off of parole five months prior to being arrested. When I heard the amount of time that my friend was sentenced to, I wasn't surprised, because I knew he had an extensive background for drugs and the laws are simply too harsh for drugs. I was definitely hurt, because I knew that there was a part of him that wanted to change, but resisted because it was too unfamiliar and the thought of working all week for a lousy paycheck, just didn't make financial sense (cents) to him.

Trust and believe, I know what it feels like when you're used to making thousands of dollars a week and being reduced to a sorry paycheck of only a few hundred dollars. I know what it feels like to work and get your paycheck, pay bills, and then be left with barely enough to hold you over until the following week. There were times when I had to dish out my ENTIRE check for bills one week and dish out my ENTIRE check the following week to get renovations done at my bookstore. The whole process of putting money into a business that wasn't making me any money was tough. Just fighting to get to the finish was a long and tedious process. It was very hurtful because I went weeks without having extra money to enjoy myself and treat myself to anything. What kept me going was the fact that I could increase my finances. One of the things that gave me joy was the fact that I didn't take any shortcuts in order to reach my goals. It is my belief that as we mature in our thinking as adults and business people, we don't intentionally put ourselves in positions to lose. It's about

78

putting ourselves at a vantage point, and whenever you resort to illegal activity, you're always at a disadvantage point.

Let's look at things from a numerical viewpoint. It's at least a 30% chance that you'll be robbed (and we know that the likely percent is actually higher)and at least a 55% that you'll get busted by the police and another 5% chance that you'll be murdered or will end up murdering someone. That's why Author Akbar Pray, who was unjustly sentenced to life in prison on drug charges said in his book in reference to street life: "Shawty you haven't entered a game, you've entered a trap." By gambling with at least 90% of the odds working against you, you're definitely in a trap. I'll be the first to admit that I had some real growing up to do to come to this realization. We have to stop chasing crazy odds and hoping to make a few dollars in exchange for our lives. The real point that I'm trying to make here is this, "It's not even worth taking the chance, your life is definitely worth too much value. YOU MATTER. YOUR LIFE MATTERS."

I need you to know and understand that there's many

ways to generate money other than resorting to the streets. I sold drugs for over 25 years and I did it in nine different states. So, I totally understand the desire to change, but being resistant to change, because of the mere thought of not being able to supplement the quantity of drug money that one may be accustomed to getting. I'm here to let it be known that you can still get the kind of money that you were used to getting from the streets, it's just a matter of working hard and making sacrifices. You have to be willing to work hard and make sacrifices in order to save enough so that you can make some wise investment choices. However, please know that you have to be extremely patient throughout this process, because it's not going to happen overnight. I know that the being patient part is tough for most dudes that hustled in the streets, because we've gotten used to immediate gratification. However, you can build yourself a legal financial fortune, but you have to be willing to be patient. While you're being patient and working diligently to bring your plans to fruition, keep in mind that sky scrapers are built one brick at a time.

It may take some time to accomplish your goals, but as long as you make constant progress, it's all good. I reopened my bookstore, started a real estate company and released this book through my own publishing company. Therefore, understand that it was a long and grueling task with each business, but I persevered, because the streets weren't an option for me. The real message that I'm trying to convey here is that I made it all happen off of a ten dollar per hour job. I cut no corners; I simply put in the blood, sweat, and work that was needed to get to the finish line. I knew beforehand as I formed the vision in my mind that it wasn't going to be easy, but I also told myself that easy was not an option. You have to continuously remind yourself that the attainment of your goals won't be easy and to keep pushing forward despite any obstacles or opposition that you encounter along the way. I wish I could tell you that the journey to achieving your goals is going to be paved with joy and an abundance of money, but that wouldn't be realistic. The truth of the matter is this: The journey is definitely going to have a great deal of pain and a shortage of money and there's more than likely going to be times when you're probably going to want to throw in the towel. However, I'm telling you from experience, "Don't give up and don't give in." There were times when things got tough for me and I had to replay the wisdom of T.D. Jakes' words over in my head to serve as inspiration to keep pushing forward. T.D. Jakes said, "You'll face your greatest opposition right before the breakthrough." You'll have to feed your mind daily with positive affirmations, because quitting is not an option. You can win righteously, but you have to make a declaration. With that being said, let me reiterate what I said a few lines earlier about when those tough times show up, "Don't give up and Don't give in." It's time for me to bring this part to an end, but I will close on this note

One of the worst disservices that we can do to ourselves is to allow our deep rooted criminal thinking to have us rotting away in a jail cell knowing that we never gave ourselves an honest chance.

GIVE YOURSELF PERMISSION TO SUCCEED BY GIVING YOURSELF AN HONEST CHANCE.
-   Jemell "Casper" Hill

TEAMSUCCESS PUBLICATIONS

WWW.FACEBOOK.COM/CASPER.HILL.12

WWW.INSTAGRAM.COM/AUTHOR_CASPERHILL

TEAMSUCCESS PUBLICATIONS, LLC – PO BOX 2553 – YORK, PA 17405

FROM
D.O.C.
TO
C.E.O.